POLAR ANIMALS
LIFE IN THE FREEZER

MUSK OXEN

by Ruth Owen

WINDMILL
BOOKS ™

New York

Published in 2013 by Windmill Books, An Imprint of Rosen Publishing
29 East 21st Street, New York, NY 10010

Produced for Windmill by Ruby Tuesday Books Ltd
Editor for Ruby Tuesday Books Ltd: Mark J. Sachner
US Editor: Sara Antill
Designer: Emma Randall
Consultant: Brad Shults, Wildlife Biologist, National Park Service

Photo Credits:
Cover, 7, 8, 11, 16, 19, 24-25, 26-27 © Shutterstock; 4, 12-13, 17 © istockphoto; 5, 6-7, 9, 10, 14-15, 18, 20-21, 22-23, 29 © FLPA; 27 (top) © Mark Austin, Musk Ox Development Corporation.

Library of Congress Cataloging-in-Publication Data

Owen, Ruth, 1967–
 Musk oxen / by Ruth Owen.
     p. cm. — (Polar animals: life in the freezer)
 Includes index.
 ISBN 978-1-4777-0219-2 (library binding) — ISBN 978-1-4777-0225-3 (pbk.) —
 ISBN 978-1-4777-0226-0 (6-pack)
 1. Muskox—Juvenile literature. I. Title.
 QL737.U53O94 2013
 599.64'78—dc23
                                        2012020685

Manufactured in the United States of America

CPSIA Compliance Information: Batch # BW13WM: For Further Information contact Windmill Books, New York, New York at 1-866-478-0556

CONTENTS

AN ARCTIC SURVIVOR

A herd of giant, shaggy oxen move slowly over an open, ice-covered landscape. Fierce winds blow, and the temperature is way below freezing. Battling the weather alongside the oxen is a family of huge woolly mammoths. This is survival in the **Arctic** during the last **Ice Age**.

Fast forward 20,000 years to the present day. The woolly mammoths are no longer around. The huge, shaggy musk oxen, however, still roam the windswept, icy Arctic **tundra**.

Musk oxen have lived for thousands of years in one of the coldest, toughest **environments** on Earth. Today, these animals are still thriving. They battle the Arctic cold and winds, and amazingly survive life in the freezer.

A musk ox

An adult male musk ox

Inuit people in Alaska who speak the Inupiat language call the musk ox "oomingmak." It means "bearded one" in Inupiat.

Beard

THE LAND OF THE MUSK OX

The Arctic tundra, the home of musk oxen, is one of the harshest **habitats** on Earth.

No trees or large plants with long roots can grow on the rocky tundra because the land is covered with just 3 feet (1 m) of soil. Below this top layer of soil are hundreds of feet (m) of permanently frozen ground, called **permafrost**.

In summer, temperatures can reach 60°F (16°C) on the Arctic tundra. In winter, however, they may drop to -40°F (-40°C)!

A herd of musk oxen on the tundra in winter

It's not just the cold and lack of soil that makes it difficult for plants to grow here. Icy winds blow over the tundra at up to 60 miles per hour (97 km/h). Only low-growing plants with short roots, such as grasses and mosses, survive in this habitat.

For much of the year, the tundra and its plant life are covered with ice or snow. During the 50 to 60 days of Arctic summer, however, the ice and snow melt. Then wildflowers and other plants burst into life.

Musk oxen on the tundra in summer

LIFE ON THE TUNDRA

Musk oxen roam the Arctic tundra in herds. A herd usually has around 20 members, but it may contain as many as 75 animals.

A herd includes adult males, adult females and their calves, and young, or juvenile, males and females.

The tundra may be a tough place to live, but it is not just musk oxen that survive in this environment. Musk oxen's neighbors include caribou and smaller animals, such as arctic foxes, wolverines, hares, and lemmings.

Polar bears, wolves, and bears are the Arctic's top **predators**. These large meat-eaters sometimes attack and kill a young, very old, or sick musk ox.

Caribou

Wolverine

Arctic fox

Grizzly bear

Wolves

Polar bear

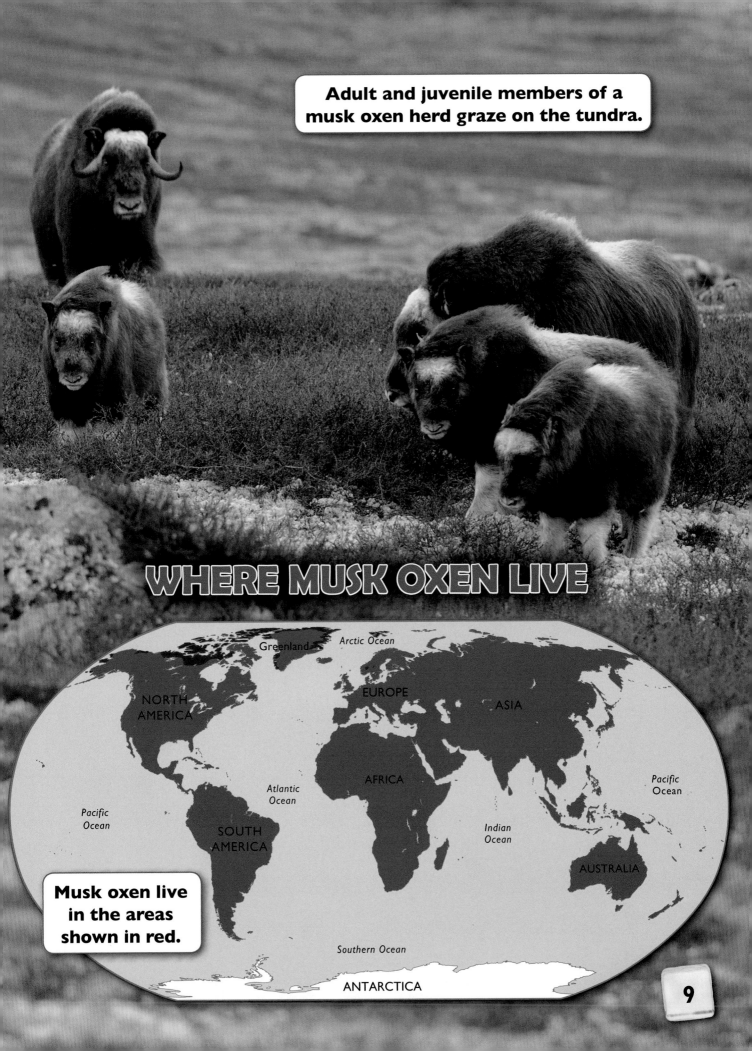

Adult and juvenile members of a musk oxen herd graze on the tundra.

WHERE MUSK OXEN LIVE

Greenland
Arctic Ocean

NORTH AMERICA

EUROPE

ASIA

Atlantic Ocean

AFRICA

Pacific Ocean

Pacific Ocean

SOUTH AMERICA

Indian Ocean

Pacific Ocean

AUSTRALIA

Musk oxen live in the areas shown in red.

Southern Ocean

ANTARCTICA

PHYSICAL FACTS

Aside from their long, shaggy coats, one of the first things you notice about musk oxen are their spectacular horns. Both males and females have a large, curved horn on either side of their face.

Male musk oxen have larger horns than females. A male's horns also meet on his forehead to create a large solid block of horn, while a female has a hairy forehead.

Musk oxen have short legs and chunky, barrel-shaped bodies. An adult's body can be up to 7 feet (2.1 m) long. From the ground to its shoulder, a male can measure 5 feet (1.5 m) tall. A female usually grows to around 4 feet (1.2 m) tall.

Female musk oxen weigh between 400 and 500 pounds (181–227 kg). A large male may weigh up to 800 pounds (363 kg).

A female musk ox with a hairy forehead

Solid block of horn

Musk oxen get their name from the strong, musky smell of the male oxen.

A male musk ox

DESIGNED FOR COLD

Musk oxen could not survive in the Arctic's subzero temperatures without their super-thick, hairy coats. Every part of a musk ox's skin, except for its lips and nostrils, is protected from the cold by fur.

A musk ox's coat has two layers. The long, shaggy, brown outer coat is made up of tough hairs known as guard hairs.

A musk ox shedding its underfur

Long, brown guard hairs

Under the guard hairs is a woolly undercoat that grows to about 3 inches (7.6 cm) long all over the animal's body. This coat grows in the fall to keep the animal warm during the winter. The thick, soft fur is eight times warmer than sheep's wool!

In spring, the woolly undercoat falls out in large clumps. Shedding its undercoat stops a musk ox from overheating during the warmer summer months.

A musk ox's woolly undercoat is known by its Inuit name of "qiviut." When the oxen shed their coats in spring, lumps of fur get caught on bushes. Native Alaskans gather the fur and spin it into soft yarn.

Soft, woolly undercoat

FIGHTING FOR FEMALES

Adult male musk oxen are known as bulls. Musk ox herds include young bulls, old bulls, and **dominant** bulls. The dominant bulls are the strongest, healthiest males. In summer, these males begin their annual battle to win females!

Two musk ox bulls fighting

When the **mating** season arrives, a dominant bull tries to gather himself a group of about 20 females to mate with. To win his females and stop other males from stealing them away, a bull often has to fight with a rival.

The two fighting bulls charge at each other at up to 35 miles per hour (56 km/h). Their heads collide with a crash that can be heard 1 mile (1.6 km) away! Then they back up and charge again. Sometimes two bulls may charge each other up to 20 times before one bull gives in and runs away.

Bulls can be seriously injured during their head-on crashes, but most survive to fight another day. This is because their brains are protected by 3 inches (7.6 cm) of thick skull and the 4-inch- (10 cm) thick mass of horn material on their foreheads.

MOTHERS AND CALVES

In April or May, about eight months after mating, a female musk ox gives birth, usually to just one calf.

The calf struggles to get to its feet soon after it is born. Within just a few hours it is able to walk and run and keep up with the adult members of the herd. A predator could easily kill a helpless calf, so it's essential that the young animal is on its feet and on the move as quickly as possible.

For the first two months of its life, a calf feeds only on its mother's milk. Then it begins to eat plants and will only drink milk occasionally.

A female musk ox usually gives birth to a calf every year. If plant food is scarce, however, she may not have a new calf. Instead, she will save all her milk for her year-old calf to help the young animal survive the food shortage.

A female musk ox and her calf

A newborn musk ox calf weighs about 20 to 30 pounds (9–14 kg). Calves grow fast and can be ten times this weight by the time they are one year old.

A musk ox calf

THE TUNDRA MENU

Survival on the Arctic tundra is not just difficult because of the extreme cold. Finding enough food can be a battle, too.

Musk oxen eat grasses and willow plants. These foods are not very **nutritious**, and often in winter it can be difficult for these large animals to find enough to eat.

Musk oxen use their excellent sense of smell to find food under the snow. Then they dig through the snow with their hooves to get to the food. If the snow has formed a hard outer crust, the tough beasts use their heads to crash through the solid snow.

When summer comes, the tundra's plants grow fast. Then the musk oxen get to feast on new shoots, fresh grasses, and wildflowers.

A musk ox searches for food under the snow in winter.

During the summer, musk oxen eat as much as they can to build up their bodies for mating, pregnancy, and surviving the harsh winter ahead.

For a few weeks in summer, musk oxen can find plenty of plants to eat.

SURVIVAL STRATEGIES

When winter comes, musk oxen must use their survival skills to find food and beat the cold.

Digging for food under the snow can use up a lot of energy, so musk oxen spend the winter in areas where the snow is shallow and food is easier to reach. There is one problem with this strategy, however. The reason these places have a lighter covering of snow is that fierce winds are constantly blowing the snow away. It may be easier for musk oxen to find food, but as they **forage**, they must endure freezing winds.

With limited food available, saving energy is a must for winter survival. Musk oxen spend a lot of time in the winter resting and sleeping. This allows their bodies to conserve energy for keeping warm and digging for food.

When icy winds blow and blizzards blast across the treeless tundra, there is nowhere for an animal to take shelter. Musk oxen simply lie down on the frozen ground and turn their backs to the winds!

As a blizzard rages, a musk ox searches for food.

DEFENSIVE TEAMWORK

A lone musk ox could fall prey to a grizzly bear or a pack of wolves. When a herd works together to defend each other, however, it is very difficult for a predator to make a kill.

When a predator approaches a herd of musk oxen, the animals face the enemy and form a line with their bodies tightly packed together. Confronted with a line of powerful animals with large horns, the predator usually chooses not to attack.

If a pack of wolves tries to surround the herd, the musk oxen form a tightly packed circle with their heads facing outward. The herd's calves huddle together safe inside the circle of giant adult bodies. Again, a predator faced with a ring of giant horned heads usually decides to find an easier meal elsewhere!

Sometimes one musk ox may break out of the defensive line or circle to charge a predator. It quickly takes its place, though, back in formation after it has made its charge.

A herd of musk oxen in a defensive line

AN AMAZING JOURNEY

Musk oxen had lived in Alaska for tens of thousands of years. By the late 1800s, however, they were **extinct** in this part of the world.

Scientists don't know for sure why musk oxen died out in Alaska at this time. Part of the reason was overhunting by people. Changes in this region's **climate** may also have affected the animals over time.

In 1930, the United States Congress put in place a plan to return the musk ox to Alaska. A herd of 34 animals were captured in Greenland and transported by ship to Norway. From there, the animals crossed the Atlantic

Ocean by ship to New York. Then the huge, woolly travelers were taken west by train to Seattle. From Seattle they sailed by ship to Alaska, finally reaching their new home in a forest in Fairbanks, about 8,000 miles (12,875 km) from where they were born.

Five years later, the herd was taken by ship along the Yukon River and over the Bering Sea to the island of Nunivak. The animals have thrived, and today there are around 500 musk oxen living on Nunivak.

Musk oxen from Nunivak have been moved to other parts of Alaska, such as Nelson Island and the Seward Peninsula. Some animals were also taken to Russia.

An adult and two young musk oxen

MUSK OXEN AND HUMANS

Early humans ate the meat of musk oxen and used their fur and skins to make clothes and shelters. The animals' horns were used to make tools and were also carved into decorative craft items.

In the spring, the musk oxen on the Musk Ox Farm have their underfur combed from their bodies so it can be used to make yarn. Up to 7 pounds (3.2 kg) of fur can be harvested from an adult animal.

Musk oxen on a farm

Musk oxen are still a source of food for some native communities in the Arctic today. The musk oxen's fur, or qiviut, is also an important source of income for some native Alaskans.

In 1964, the Musk Ox Project began in Fairbanks, Alaska. The Musk Ox Farm was set up to breed and raise oxen so that their fur could be harvested. Local women were then taught how to spin and knit the wool to create beautiful qiviut garments, which could be sold. By the 1970s, hundreds of women were earning money through the project, and it is still going strong today.

Musk ox underfur called qiviut

THE FUTURE FOR MUSK OXEN

Today, musk oxen's numbers are strong and the animals are not in danger. **Climate change**, however, could be a threat to the musk ox in the future.

Warmer winters can cause snow to thaw or rain to fall in the Arctic. Then, when temperatures drop again, the rainwater or melted snow freezes, locking the animals' food under deep ice. As Arctic temperatures increase, the tundra habitat could change. Over time, the tundra plants that musk oxen eat might be replaced by forests.

While trees on the tundra and warmer winters might seem like a good thing, musk oxen and other Arctic animals are not designed to live in this type of climate or habitat. Only time will tell how climate change will affect these animals.

For now, icy winds blow and blizzards rage, but the tough musk oxen continue to survive in their Arctic home as they have done for thousands of years.

Scientists estimate that there are around 130,000 musk oxen in the world today.

29

GLOSSARY

Arctic (ARK-tik)
The northernmost area on Earth, which includes northern parts of Europe, Asia, and North America, the Arctic Ocean, the polar ice cap, and the North Pole.

climate (KLY-mut)
The average temperature and weather in an area over a period of 30 or more years.

climate change (KLY-mut CHAYNJ)
The slow warming of planet Earth. Climate change is happening because gases from burning fuels such as coal and oil gather high above the planet and trap the Sun's heat.

dominant (DAH-mih-nent)
Most important and successful.

environment (en-VY-ern-ment) All the living things and conditions of a place.

extinct (ik-STINGKT)
No longer existing.

forage (FOR-ij)
To move from place to place looking for food.

habitat (HA-buh-tat)
The place where an animal or plant normally lives. A habitat may be a rain forest, the ocean, or a backyard.

Ice Age (EYES AYJ)
A long period of time when the temperatures of Earth and its atmosphere drop, causing huge glaciers, or sheets of ice, to form across the land.

mating (MAYT-ing)
Coming together in order to have young.

nutritious
(noo-TRIH-shus)
Containing nutrients, such as vitamins, that a body needs to help it live and grow.

permafrost (PUR-muh-frost)
A layer of soil below the surface that is always frozen.

predator
(PREH-duh-ter)
An animal that hunts and kills other animals for food.

tundra (TUN-druh)
A rocky, treeless, boggy landscape of low-growing plants. Below the surface is a layer of permanently frozen soil called permafrost.

Websites

For web resources related to the subject of this book, go to: www.windmillbooks.com/weblinks and select this book's title.

READ MORE

Lynette, Rachel. *Who Lives on the Cold, Icy Tundra?*. Exploring Habitats. New York: PowerKids Press, 2011.

Markle, Sandra. *Musk Oxen*. Animal Prey. Minneapolis, MN: Lerner Publications Company, 2007.

Patrick, Roman. *Musk Oxen*. Animals That Live in the Tundra. New York: Gareth Stevens, 2011.

INDEX